CAPRICORN:

A COMPLETE GUIDE TO THE CAPRICORN ASTROLOGY STAR SIGN

Sofia Visconti

Contents

INTRODUCTION

Astrology, with a history spanning thousands of years, goes beyond being a mystical art form. This practice is based on the belief that the arrangement of stars and planets has an impact on lives by shaping our characters, influencing our emotions and potentially guiding our paths. It connects the positions of bodies at the time of our birth to different aspects of our personality, life experiences and even our destiny. At its core astrology aims to comprehend the relationships between the universe and our earthly existence. By studying how celestial bodies move, astrologers interpret meanings. From this they can gain insights into various facets of life including personal relationships, career decisions and much more.

Each astrological sign within the Zodiac represents a collection of traits and tendencies that influences individuals born under that sign. This book focuses on exploring the zodiac sign, Capricorn. Our goal is to provide a deep dive into Capricorn. By merging ancient knowledge with contemporary perspectives this book will explore the ways in which Capricorns interact with the world, their strengths, challenges, how they can utilize their traits, compatibility and much more. Whether you happen to be a Capricorn seeking self discovery, someone close to a Capricorn or simply an astrology enthusiast this book guarantees fresh insights and a profound comprehension.

OVERVIEW OF THE CAPRICORN ZODIAC SIGN

- **Date of Star Sign:** Capricorn, the tenth sign in the Zodiac, encompasses those born between December 22nd and January 19th. This period marks the transition from the end of one year to the beginning of the next. It symbolizes a time of reflection and resolution.

- **Symbol:** The symbol of Capricorn is the Sea-Goat. It is a mythical creature with the body of a goat and the tail of a fish. This symbol represents Capricorn's ability to thrive both in the material world (the goat, climbing to the highest mountains) and in the emotional realm (the fish, swimming in the deepest waters), showcasing their versatility and resilience.

- **Element:** Earth is the element associated with Capricorn. Capricorns are known for their pragmatic approach to life. Earth elements ground them, endowing them with a sense of stability, practicality and realism.

- **Planet**: Saturn, the planet of discipline and responsibility, rules Capricorn. This association highlights their structured, ambitious and persevering nature. Saturn's influence is seen in the Capricorn's penchant for setting long-term goals and their determination in achieving them.
- **Color**: The color most often linked with Capricorn is dark brown or gray, reflecting their serious, earthbound and resilient nature.
- **Personality Traits**: Capricorns are known for their discipline, ambition and hardworking nature. They also hold a strong sense of duty and responsibility. While sometimes seen as reserved or cautious, they also possess a dry wit and understated charm.
- **Strengths**: Among their strengths are determination, strong will and the ability to plan and execute long-term projects. Their practicality and reliability make them excellent leaders and trusted advisors. Loyalty and a deep sense of commitment are also hallmark strengths of a Capricorn.
- **Weaknesses**: Their weaknesses might include a tendency towards pessimism or cynicism, being overly reserved or distant and sometimes struggling with stubbornness. Capricorns tend to also be overly concerned with their public image. As such they may fear failure or ridicule.
- **Compatibility**: Capricorns often find the most harmony in relationships with Taurus and Virgo, earth signs that share their practical outlook on life. They also can have strong connections with water signs like Scorpio and Pisces. These can bring

emotional depth and balance to the practicality of Capricorn.

In the introduction of this book we have embarked on a captivating journey into the realm of astrology with a focus on the intriguing and ambitious nature of Capricorn individuals. The introduction sets the stage for an exploration of this star sign renowned for its practicality, discipline and strong sense of responsibility. As readers progress through this book they can expect an exploration of many aspects that contribute to the Capricorn personality.

- **In Depth Character Analysis**; A close examination, into typical behavioral patterns, emotional landscape and intellectual traits that shape Capricorns.
- **Historical and Cultural Perspectives**; Delve into the cultural interpretations of Capricorn. Gain an understanding of this astrological sign through diverse perspectives across time.
- **Understanding Capricorn in Relationships;** Discover the dynamics of relationships involving Capricorns. Plus insights into their compatibility with other zodiac signs and tips for fostering harmonious connections.
- **Career and Ambitions;** Explore how Capricorns unique traits shape their lives and aspirations. Discover strategies for maximizing their strengths in the workplace.
- **Overcoming Challenges and Personal Growth;** Uncover the challenges faced by Capricorns. Learn strategies for personal growth, overcoming obstacles and tapping into their full potential.

- **Real life Stories and Experiences;** Hear narratives from individuals who were born under the Capricorn sign. Gain practical insights that resonate with real world experiences.
- **Practical Tips for a Balanced Life;** Discover life advice catered to Capricorns on achieving balance, wellness and fulfillment in various aspects of life.
- All of this and much, much more.

Overall this comprehensive guide is designed to provide an in-depth understanding of the Capricorn sign. Whether you are a Capricorn yourself or one who has connections with one. Or if you're simply having an interest in astrology. This journey of exploration promises wisdom, self reflection and a greater appreciation for this remarkable star sign.

CHAPTER 1:
HISTORY AND MYTHOLOGY

I n this chapter we embark on a captivating journey, through the ages to explore the history and mythology surrounding the Capricorn zodiac sign. With its representation as the sea goat Capricorn, has captivated people's imaginations across numerous cultures and time periods. Here we unveil the tapestry of stories, beliefs and historical events that have shaped how we understand and appreciate Capricorn throughout history.

We begin our exploration by delving into the ancient origins of the Capricorn constellation. Let us trace its observations and recordings in ancient civilizations such as Babylon, Greece and Rome. These initial discoveries lay the foundation for comprehending how diverse cultures worldwide have perceived, represented and integrated Capricorn into their mythological frameworks.

As we delve deeper into mythology we encounter enchanting tales associated with Capricorn that offer fresh insights into nature and cosmic order. From captivating stories about the Greek god Pan's adventures, to nurturing accounts featuring Amalthea the goat associated with Zeus. These mythological narratives provide a glimpse into attempts to comprehend and personify forces and destiny.

Advancing through time we highlight events and noteworthy individuals born under this sign who have influenced history. Additionally we take a moment to contemplate the changing perception of Capricorn over time. This part offers an overview of how our understanding of Capricorn has evolved from celestial interpretations to a more contemporary approach that focuses on psychology and individual personality traits. Let's begin our journey through time.

HISTORICAL AND MYTHOLOGICAL ORIGINS

The constellation of Capricorn, known for its distinctive sea-goat symbol, holds a rich history that dates back to some of the earliest civilizations. The story of Capricorn begins with ancient sky-watchers who first observed this constellation in the night sky.

BABYLONIAN ASTRONOMY

One of the earliest known records of the Capricorn constellation comes from the Babylonians. They observed it as early as the 2nd millennium BC and named it "Suhur-mash-ha," the "Goat-Fish," due to its symbolic representation of a creature that was half goat and half fish. This depiction was likely influenced by the ancient god Enki, a deity associated with water, knowledge and creation. It was often depicted with a goat-like upper body and a fish-like lower body.

ANCIENT GREECE

In ancient Greek mythology, Capricorn is often linked to the story of the god Pan, who transformed into a half-goat, half-fish creature to escape the monster Typhon. Another Greek myth connects Capricorn to Amalthea, the goat who nursed the infant Zeus, and whose horn was transformed into the "Cornucopia" or "horn of plenty."

ROMAN INFLUENCE

The Romans adopted this constellation into their astrology and integrated it into their mythological tapestry. Capricornus, as it was known in Latin, maintained its significance as a symbol of duality and resourcefulness.

ANCIENT CHINA

In Chinese astronomy, the stars of Capricorn were associated with the water element. These were a part of different constellations that depicted mythical creatures and important figures in Chinese mythology.

INDIAN ASTRONOMY

In Indian astrology, which predates Western astrology, the region of the sky corresponding to Capricorn is known as "Makara." This is a term that also refers to a mythical sea creature. One that is similar to the sea-goat of Western astrology.

ARABIAN ASTRONOMY

In Arabian astronomy, the constellation was seen as a part of larger figures or stories, often blending with their rich tradition of storytelling and sky interpretation.

INDIGENOUS CULTURES

Various indigenous cultures around the world had their interpretations and stories related to the stars of Capricorn, often reflecting their environment, traditions and beliefs.

Throughout history and across cultures the constellation of Capricorn has held an important place in our collective imagination. It has been depicted in stories and symbols that transcend time and geographic boundaries. Each culture's interpretation of Capricorn reflects its values, mythology and understanding of the universe contributing to the diverse history of this celestial formation.

In ancient times Capricorn was often associated with gods and mythical creatures reflecting the beliefs and knowledge about the cosmos prevalent during those eras. In modern astrology there has been a shift from mythological interpretations to psychological insights. Astrology is now commonly used as a tool for self reflection and a way of understanding one's personality traits. We now explore the traits of Capricorns in terms of how they influence our choices, relationships and life journeys.

HISTORICAL EVENTS UNDER THE CAPRICORN SEASON

The Capricorn season, spanning from December 22nd to January 19th, has been a period marked by several significant historical events.

- **Historical Events:** Throughout history, many pivotal events have occurred during the Capricorn season. The signing of important treaties and declarations and significant scientific breakthroughs have often coincided with this period. These events, in astrological terms, could be seen as reflections of Capricorn's traits of determination and groundbreaking ambition.
- **Global Celebrations and Shifts:** Many global celebrations and shifts, including the start of a new year, occur during the Capricorn season. These transitions and celebrations might be viewed as symbolic of the Capricorn's affinity for reflection, planning and setting ambitious goals for the future.

HISTORICAL FIGURES BORN UNDER THE CAPRICORN SIGN

- **Leaders and States Persons**: Many influential leaders and states persons were born under the Capricorn sign. They are known for their strategic thinking and leadership qualities. Figures such as Martin Luther King Jr, Benjamin Franklin, and Muhammad Ali exemplify Capricorn traits. That is through their impactful contributions to society in their respective fields.

- **Scientists and Innovators**: The discipline and dedication of Capricorns have been embodied in several renowned scientists and innovators like Isaac Newton, whose birthday falls under this sign. Their contributions have significantly advanced human knowledge and understanding.

As we come to the end of this chapter, let us take a moment to reflect on the stories, significant events and influential individuals linked to this enduring zodiac sign. From its ancient origins to its relevance in modern astrology Capricorn has consistently represented ambition, discipline and a practical approach to life's obstacles. In a world that is constantly changing the traits associated with Capricorn, determination, responsibility and practical wisdom remain as relevant as ever.

FURTHER READING AND REFERENCES

For readers interested in delving deeper into the history, mythology and contemporary understanding of Capricorn, the following list of primary sources, ancient texts, and modern writings is recommended:

- **"Hamlet's Mill: An Essay Investigating the Origins of Human Knowledge and Its Transmission Through Myth "** by Giorgio de Santillana and Hertha von Dechend: This work explores the connections between ancient myths and the astronomical knowledge of the time. Context on mythological origins of constellations, such as Capricorn are included.

- **"The Fables of Hyginus"** translated by Mary Grant: This classical text includes stories from Greek and Roman mythology. Insights into the mythological background of the Capricorn constellation are included.
- **"Capricorn": The Art of Living Well and Finding Happiness According to Your Star Sign"** by Sally Kirkman: This contemporary book offers a focused look at the Capricorn sign. Inside it discusses how its traits can be harnessed for personal growth and happiness.
- **"Saturn: A New Look at an Old Devil"** by Liz Greene: This book delves into the influence of Saturn, the ruling planet of Capricorn, in astrology. Insights into how its positioning can affect personality and life events are included.
- **"Astrology, History, and Apocalypse"** by Nicholas Campion: This text provides a historical overview of astrology. It includes the evolution of the interpretation of zodiac signs like Capricorn.
- **Online resources such as The Astrological Association and The American Federation of Astrologers** - These offer a wealth of articles, research papers, and historical texts related to astrology and specific zodiac signs.

CHAPTER 2:
LOVE & COMPATIBILITY

C apricorn is commonly associated with a calm demeanor, unwavering focus on goals and a practical outlook on life. However beneath their reserved exterior lies an realm characterized by profound loyalty, unwavering commitment and an aspiration for long lasting connections. This chapter seeks to illuminate the nuances of Capricorns love life. From their approach to dating and courtship to their compatibility with each zodiac sign.

Firstly we will examine the traits that define Capricorn's experience in love. From how they express affection. To what they seek in a partner and the nuanced ways in which they navigate relationships. Understanding all of this is vital, for appreciating the profoundness of their bonds. Subsequently we will explore the compatibility between Capricorn and the other zodiac signs. We'll delve into the dynamics of each pairing highlighting their strengths and challenges. From the passion of Aries to the depths of Pisces these combinations offer a unique mix of energies, lessons and experiences.

This in depth exploration isn't just for Capricorns and their potential partners. It's also for anyone interested in astrology and the enigmatic world of love. And of course, whether you're a Capricorn looking to understand your nature or a partner seeking to deepen your bond with a

Capricorn this chapter will provide guidance and insight. So let's embark on this journey of discovery together as we uncover the secrets of Capricorn's heart and unravel the dance that defines their relationships.

CAPRICORN'S APPROACH TO LOVE AND ROMANCE

When it comes to love and romance, individuals born under the Capricorn sign often exhibit a unique blend of traits that shape their approach to relationships. As an earth sign ruled by Saturn, Capricorns are known for their pragmatic, disciplined, and patient nature. Such traits are reflected in their romantic lives.

- **Slow and Steady**: Capricorns tend to take a cautious and slow approach to romance. They are not known for diving headfirst into relationships. No, instead, they prefer to take their time. They value getting to know their partner and building a foundation of trust and respect before fully committing. This gradual progression ensures that when a Capricorn commits, they are in it for the long haul.

- **Seeking Stability**: Stability and security are paramount to Capricorns in love. They are drawn to partners who are reliable, responsible and have their lives in order. For Capricorns, a stable and predictable relationship is often more appealing. Rather than a whirlwind romance filled with uncertainties.

- **Practical Expressions of Love**: Capricorns express their love in practical ways. Rather than grand gestures or overly sentimental expressions, they show their affection through acts of service, support and loyalty. They are the ones who will remember to do the little things. Things that make their partner's life easier and more comfortable.

- **Ambition and Partnership**: Capricorns are ambitious. As such they appreciate a partner who shares their drive and work ethic. They respect independence and ambition in a partner. They often seek relationships where both individuals can support and motivate each other to achieve their goals.

- **Deep Emotional Reserve**: While they may appear reserved or stoic, Capricorns possess a deep well of emotion. However, they often keep their feelings guarded until they feel completely secure in a relationship. Although once committed, they are deeply loyal and make for a dependable partner.

- **Traditional Values**: Many Capricorns lean towards traditional values when it comes to love and relationships. They appreciate the rituals of dating and courtship. As such they often adhere to conventional relationship milestones.

- **Long-Term Perspective**: Capricorns think long-term and are often planning for the future. In relationships, this means they are always considering how their partner fits into their long-term life plan. This makes them more selective about entering into a romantic commitment.

In summary, Capricorns approach love and romance with the same seriousness and dedication that they apply to other areas of their life. They value stability, practicality and loyalty. Once they find the right partner, they are committed and dependable lovers. While they may take their time to open up emotionally, their deep commitment and steady approach make them reliable and devoted partners.

CAPRICORN'S COMPATIBILITY WITH OTHER ZODIAC SIGNS

Capricorns, known for their discipline and ambition, approach relationships with seriousness and a focus on long-term goals. Let's explore how Capricorn pairs with each zodiac sign.

CAPRICORN AND ARIES

- Compatibility: Moderate to Challenging.
- Dynamics: Aries' impulsiveness clashes with Capricorn's cautious approach. However, both share a drive for success and can motivate each other.
- Challenges: Aries may find Capricorn too reserved. Capricorn might view Aries as too reckless.
- Strengths: If they can balance each other out, they can make a powerful team. Aries brings enthusiasm and Capricorn brings structure.

CAPRICORN AND TAURUS

- Compatibility: High.
- Dynamics: Both are earth signs, valuing security and stability. They share a practical approach to life and love.
- Strengths: Their shared values and goals can create a strong foundation for a lasting relationship.

- Challenges: They need to be wary of becoming too comfortable and avoid a lack of dynamism in the relationship.

CAPRICORN AND GEMINI

- Compatibility: Moderate.
- Dynamics: Gemini's social and adaptable nature can clash with Capricorn's more introverted and structured approach.
- Strengths: Gemini can introduce variety and excitement to Capricorn's life. Capricorn can offer Gemini stability.
- Challenges: Remember their different approaches to life can lead to misunderstandings. Communication is key.

CAPRICORN AND CANCER

- Compatibility: High.
- Dynamics: Opposites in the zodiac, they attract each other with their different yet complementary qualities.
- Strengths: Capricorn provides security that Cancer craves. Cancer brings emotional depth to the relationship.
- Challenges: They need to understand and respect their differing emotional needs and communication styles.

CAPRICORN AND LEO

- Compatibility: Moderate.
- Dynamics: Leo's flamboyance can clash with Capricorn's understated approach. Both are leaders, which can lead to power struggles.
- Strengths: If they align their goals, they can be a dynamic and successful pair.
- Challenges: They must learn to share the spotlight and respect each other's different styles.

CAPRICORN AND VIRGO

- Compatibility: Very High.
- Dynamics: Both are earth signs. Both share a practical approach to life and a strong work ethic.
- Strengths: They understand each other's needs for stability. As such they can build a harmonious and efficient life together.
- Challenges: They need to ensure their shared life doesn't become too routine and devoid of spontaneity.

CAPRICORN AND LIBRA

- Compatibility: Moderate.
- Dynamics: Libra's love for harmony and social interaction might conflict with Capricorn's more solitary and pragmatic nature.
- Strengths: They can complement each other well. Libra brings a sense of balance and Capricorn provides stability.

- Challenges: They need to work on understanding and valuing their different approaches to life and relationships.

CAPRICORN AND SCORPIO

- Compatibility: High.
- Dynamics: Both signs are known for their intensity and depth. They share a strong determination and commitment.
- Strengths: A deep, often unspoken understanding can develop, leading to a powerful emotional and practical bond.
- Challenges: Both need to be mindful of their tendencies towards control and stubbornness.

CAPRICORN AND SAGITTARIUS

- Compatibility: Moderate.
- Dynamics: Sagittarius' love for adventure may seem frivolous to a practical Capricorn. Conversely, Capricorn's seriousness can dampen Sagittarius's spirit.
- Strengths: They can learn a lot from each other. Sagittarius adds fun. Capricorn adds structure.
- Challenges: Finding a balance between freedom and responsibility is key to this pairing.

CAPRICORN AND CAPRICORN

- Compatibility: High.
- Dynamics: They share similar values, goals and approaches to life.
- Strengths: This pair can build a successful, stable life, by understanding each other's ambitions and work ethic.
- Challenges: They need to avoid becoming too focused on work and material success. Remember to not neglect emotional and romantic needs.

CAPRICORN AND AQUARIUS

- Compatibility: Moderate.
- Dynamics: Aquarius' unconventional nature can be intriguing yet baffling to traditional Capricorn.
- Strengths: They can both offer a different perspective. Aquarius brings innovation. Capricorn provides practicality.

- Challenges: They must learn to appreciate their differing approaches to life and freedom.

CAPRICORN AND PISCES

- Compatibility: High.
- Dynamics: Pisces' emotional depth and intuition complement Capricorn's practicality and stability.
- Strengths: Pisces can help Capricorn to relax and open up emotionally. Capricorn can provide Pisces with stability and direction.
- Challenges: They need to balance Capricorn's need for structure with Pisces' need for emotional and creative space.

In summary, Capricorn's approach to love and compatibility varies significantly across the zodiac. While they tend to form the strongest connections with earth and water signs, the potential for a fulfilling relationship exists with any sign. Ultimately, that is provided there is mutual understanding and respect.

DATING AND RELATIONSHIPS WITH CAPRICORN INDIVIDUALS

Capricorns, known for their pragmatic and disciplined approach to life, can be deeply rewarding partners. However, understanding and respecting their unique traits is key to building a strong and lasting relationship. Here are some tips tailored for both men and women when dating and having relationships with Capricorn individuals.

FOR DATING CAPRICORN MEN

- **Appreciate His Ambitions:** Capricorn men are often career-oriented and ambitious. Show interest in his goals and support his aspirations.
- **Be Patient**: He may take time to open up emotionally. Patience is crucial in allowing the relationship to develop at a pace comfortable for him.
- **Respect His Space:** Capricorn men value their personal space and time. Respecting this need can help build trust and understanding.
- **Embrace Traditional Courtship:** Many Capricorn men appreciate traditional dating rituals. Planning thoughtful dates and respecting courtship norms can be appealing to them.
- **Be Honest and Direct:** They prefer straightforward communication. Be open and honest about your feelings and intentions.
- **Show Your Practical Side:** Demonstrating your practical and sensible side can be attractive, as they value responsibility and reliability.
- **Understand His Reserved Nature**: He may not be the most outwardly expressive partner. Understanding and respecting his more reserved nature is key.

FOR DATING CAPRICORN WOMEN

- **Respect Her Independence:** Capricorn women are often independent and self-reliant. Showing respect for her autonomy is important.

- **Be Genuine**: Authenticity is important to Capricorn women. Be yourself and be genuine.
- **Stability is Key**: They are attracted to stability and security. Being reliable and stable in your actions and emotions can go a long way.
- **Appreciate Her Traditional Values**: Many Capricorn women value tradition and may appreciate conventional gestures of romance.
- **Support Her Career Goals**: Capricorn women are often career-driven. Supporting her ambitions and understanding her work commitments is crucial.
- **Patience with Emotional Openness**: She may take time to show her emotional side. Be patient and give her space to open up at her own pace.
- **Quality Time Matters**: Quality over quantity is important. Plan meaningful dates or activities that align with her interests.

Overall building and maintaining relationships with Capricorn partners require being mindful of key elements. Whether you are dating a man or woman born under the sign of Capricorn, understanding their personality traits while respecting their approach to life can foster a fulfilling and enduring relationship. Patience, supportiveness and reliability are just some of the key elements in building a bond with a Capricorn partner.

As we near the end of this chapter where we have gained a deep understanding of the romantic world experienced by those who are born under the Capricorn sign. Throughout this exploration we have delved into the depths of Capricorn's heart exploring their approach to love, how they express affection uniquely and how they find harmony with zodiac signs.

We have observed that Capricorns, with their disciplined demeanor and ambitious nature, bring a sense of seriousness and depth to their endeavors. Love for them is a process of trust building and respect forming a foundation upon which any committed relationship can thrive. In their quest for love Capricorns seek not a partner but a teammate. Someone who shares their values and comprehends their aspirations. Someone who stands unwaveringly beside them.

As we wrap up it becomes evident that comprehending and valuing the Capricorn approach to love and compatibility necessitates patience and understanding. For those romantically involved with a Capricorn, acknowledging their need for both emotional depth and practical stability can deepen the connection. For Capricorns themselves, this chapter acts as a reflection of their workings in matters of love. Lastly, we want to encourage them to embrace both their strengths and vulnerabilities in order to cultivate fulfilling relationships.

CHAPTER 3:
FRIENDS AND FAMILY

C apricorns are renowned for their positive approach to life, their sense of responsibility and an enduring loyalty. These qualities form the foundation of steady relationships. However they can also present distinctive challenges as Capricorns navigate their social and familial spheres. This chapter delves into the dynamics of how individuals born under the Capricorn sign interact, engage with others and nurture their connections. It goes beyond surface level interactions to explore the underlying currents that influence Capricorn's bonds with those closest to them. So join us as we uncover the intricacies of Capricorn's interactions within this chapter.

CAPRICORN AS A FRIEND

When it comes to friendships, individuals born under the Capricorn sign are known for their reliability, depth and loyalty. Understanding the friendship style of a Capricorn can offer insights into how they build and maintain their social connections.

- **Loyal and Trustworthy:** One of the most defining traits of a Capricorn friend is their unwavering loyalty. Once they consider someone a friend, they are often committed for life. They take their friendships seriously and are incredibly trustworthy.

- **Practical and Helpful**: Capricorns are the friends who offer practical advice and help. They are often the ones you turn to when you need a problem solved or a task accomplished. Their pragmatic approach to life makes them invaluable when it comes to giving realistic and straightforward advice.

- **Reserved but Deep:** Initially, Capricorns might come across as reserved or even aloof. However, once they open up and trust someone, they reveal a depth of character that can be both surprising and refreshing.

- **Selective with Friendships**: Capricorns tend to be selective about who they spend their time with. They prefer a small circle of close friends over a large group of acquaintances. Quality over quantity is their motto.

- **Ambitious and Motivating**: Being ambitious themselves, Capricorns are great at motivating and pushing their friends towards their goals. They are supportive and encouraging. However they also don't shy away from giving a needed reality check.

- **Appreciates Tradition**: Capricorns often have a fondness for traditions and may enjoy celebrating special occasions, anniversaries and milestones in meaningful ways with their friends.
- **Not the Most Spontaneous**: Capricorns are planners and are not known for their spontaneity. They appreciate structured activities and well-planned outings more than impromptu adventures.
- **Dependable and Consistent**: In friendships, Capricorns are incredibly dependable. You can count on them to keep their promises and be there when they say they will.
- **Values Personal Space**: They respect and value personal space. Both theirs and others. They understand and appreciate the need for alone time.
- **Long-Term Friends**: When a Capricorn invests in a friendship, it's often with a long-term view. They value and work hard to maintain lasting relationships.

In essence, a friendship with a Capricorn might take time to develop, but once it does, it often turns into a bond for life. Their loyalty, practicality and depth make them outstanding friends. Friends who provide stability and thoughtful guidance.

CAPRICORN AND FAMILY DYNAMICS

In the context of family dynamics, individuals born under the Capricorn sign often play a pivotal role. One that is characterized by their sense of responsibility, traditional values and a pragmatic approach to family matters. Understanding how Capricorns interact within the family setting reveals much about their values, priorities and the unique strengths they bring to familial relationships.

- **Responsible** Capricorns are often seen as the pillars of their families. They take their familial responsibilities seriously. Whether as parents, siblings, or children. They are the ones family members often turn to for support and guidance due to their reliable and responsible nature.

- **Traditional and Conservative**: Many Capricorns hold traditional values close to their heart. They respect family traditions and often play a key role in maintaining family customs. Be it through organizing gatherings or keeping alive certain rituals and practices.

- **Providing Stability and Security:** As natural providers, Capricorns strive to create a stable and secure environment for their family. They are often focused on ensuring that the practical needs of the family are met. From financial security to creating a structured home life.

- **Practical Problem-Solvers**: In family conflicts or challenges, Capricorns tend to be pragmatic problem-solvers. They approach issues with a level head, often helping to mediate and find practical solutions.

- **Emotional Reserve:** Capricorns can sometimes seem emotionally reserved, preferring to express their care and love through actions rather than words. Understanding their emotional style is key to appreciating the depth of their affection and commitment.
- **Strong Work Ethic:** Their strong work ethic is not just limited to their professional life. Capricorns often put in the effort to make sure their family life is running smoothly. Sometimes at the expense of their own relaxation and leisure.
- **Role Models:** Capricorns often serve as role models within the family, especially for younger members. They exemplify traits like discipline, hard work and determination.
- **Parental Approach:** As parents, Capricorns are usually strict but fair. They emphasize discipline, education and the importance of hard work. As parents they encourage their children to be independent and self-reliant.
- **Need for Personal Space:** While deeply committed to their family, Capricorns also value their personal space and time for solitude. They appreciate when this need is respected by family members.
- **Long-Term Planning:** Capricorns are often the family members who think ahead. They are likely to plan for the family's future. Whether it's saving for children's education or planning family investments.

In conclusion, Capricorns bring a sense of strength, stability and responsibility to family dynamics. Their practical nature, combined with a deep sense of duty towards family members, makes them invaluable within the family unit. Understanding and respecting their need for structure, traditional values and occasional emotional reserve can lead to harmonious family relationships.

CHALLENGES IN FRIENDSHIPS AND FAMILY RELATIONSHIPS

While Capricorns can be loyal, dependable friends and steadfast family members, they also face specific challenges in these personal relationships. Understanding these challenges can provide insights into how Capricorns navigate their social and familial worlds and how they might work towards healthier, more fulfilling relationships.

CHALLENGES IN FRIENDSHIPS

- **Difficulty in Expressing Emotions:** Capricorns are often reserved and may struggle to express their emotions openly. This can sometimes lead to misunderstandings with friends who might perceive them as aloof or uncaring.

- **Balancing Work and Social Life:** Given their ambitious nature and focus on career, Capricorns might find it challenging to balance their work life with their social commitments. Potentially this can lead to neglected friendships.

- **Reluctance to Venture Out of Comfort Zones:** Capricorns tend to stick to routines and might be hesitant to try new activities or meet new people. This can limit the expansion of their social circle.

- **High Expectations:** They often have high standards for themselves and others. This can sometimes lead to disappointment or frustration when friends don't meet these expectations.

- **Overly Cautious Approach:** Their cautious nature might make them slow to trust and open up to new friendships, potentially missing out on meaningful connections.

CHALLENGES IN FAMILY RELATIONS

- **Overly Authoritative or Controlling:** In their desire to ensure stability and security, Capricorns can come across as controlling or overly authoritative. Especially in a family setting.

- **Struggle with Work-Family Balance:** Their dedication to career and ambition can sometimes take precedence over family time. This can lead to feelings of neglect among family members.
- **Difficulty in Emotional Vulnerability:** Similar to their friendships, Capricorns may struggle to show vulnerability within their family. This can hinder deep emotional connections.
- **Resistance to Change:** Capricorns often prefer tradition and may resist changes in family dynamics or routines. This can be challenging in evolving family structures.
- **Tendency to Take on Too Much Responsibility:** They often take on the role of the provider or problem-solver in the family. This can be overwhelming and lead to stress.

To overcome these challenges Capricorns can focus on expressing their emotions honestly in both friendships and family relationships. It is important for them to find a balance between work and personal life so as to learn how to relax their high standards and control impulsive tendencies. Embracing change and new experiences can also bring fulfillment to their connections. By acknowledging and addressing these obstacles Capricorns have the potential to develop meaningful bonds with friends and family.

As we wrap up this chapter, it becomes evident that developing relationships with Capricorns, be it friendships or familial bonds, requires patience and empathy.

Acknowledging and appreciating their need for stability, respect for tradition and occasional reserved nature can contribute to rewarding connections. For Capricorns themselves, finding a balance between their sense of responsibility and the importance of vulnerability can enhance the quality of their personal relationships.

CHAPTER 4:
CAREER AND MONEY

———————— ✿ ————————

Capricorns are often propelled by a drive for success, stability and accomplishments in their careers. This chapter aims to explore the attributes that enable Capricorns to thrive in professional settings. We'll delve into their career paths and the challenges they often face on their journey towards professional excellence. Additionally we'll examine how their pragmatic and strategic nature influences decisions regarding finances, investment strategies and overall wealth management.

Come join us as we delve into the realms of careers and money, from a Capricorn's perspective. Together we will uncover their strategies, strengths and challenges that shape their unique approach to these aspects of life.

CAPRICORN CAREER PREFERENCES AND PROFESSIONAL ASPIRATIONS

Capricorns, known for their practicality, ambition and discipline, have distinct preferences when it comes to their careers. Their approach to work is often marked by determination, a strong work ethic and a focus on long-term goals. Understanding the professional world of a Capricorn reveals much about their values and what they seek in a career.

- **Structure and Stability:** Capricorns thrive in careers that offer stability and structure. They prefer well-established organizations with clear hierarchies and well defined career paths. As such they are often drawn to traditional fields like finance, management and administration where their organizational skills can be fully utilized.

- **Ambitious**: Capricorns are highly ambitious and often set lofty goals for themselves. They are willing to put in the hard work and dedication required to climb the professional ladder. Leadership roles, where they can exercise control and implement their vision, are particularly appealing to them.

- **Methodical and Detail-Oriented Approach:** They excel in careers that require attention to detail and a methodical approach. Professions in accounting, human resources and it are notable positions for them to excel in.

- **Strong Sense of Responsibility:** A strong sense of responsibility and duty often drives Capricorns in their professional choices. They are dependable and take their work commitments seriously. Overall this makes them reliable employees and managers.

- **Preference for Traditional and Practical Fields:** Capricorns often gravitate towards fields that offer tangible results and practical applications. This can include industries like construction, architecture and real estate.

- **Long-Term Career Vision:** Capricorns typically have a long-term view of their career trajectory. They like to plan their professional journey meticulously, often aiming for positions that promise higher status and security over time.

- **Need for Achievement and Recognition:** Recognition for their hard work and achievements is important to Capricorns. They strive for positions that not only offer financial rewards but also confer respect and authority.

- **Entrepreneurial Tendencies:** Some Capricorns may be drawn to entrepreneurial ventures. Their discipline and strategic planning skills make them well-suited to the challenges of starting and running a business.

- **Balancing Work with Personal Life:** Despite their career focus, Capricorns also understand the importance of balancing work with personal life. They seek careers that, while demanding, also allow them time to enjoy their personal lives.

- **Continuous Learning and Growth:** Finally, Capricorns value careers that offer opportunities for continuous learning and growth. They are always seeking to improve their skills and knowledge, often through additional training or higher education.

In conclusion, Capricorns bring a unique combination of ambition, practicality and discipline to their professional lives. They are drawn to careers that offer stability, structure and the opportunity for long-term growth. Their commitment to their work, coupled with their ability to plan and execute, often leads them to achieve high levels of success in their chosen fields.

STRENGTHS OF CAPRICORN INDIVIDUALS IN THE WORKPLACE

Capricorn individuals bring a unique set of strengths to the workplace, often propelling them to excel in their professional endeavors. Their natural traits align well with many aspects of a successful career. Overall this makes them valuable assets in various work environments. Here are some key strengths that typically allow Capricorns to thrive professionally.

- **Strong Work Ethic:** Capricorns are known for their exceptional work ethic. They are hardworking, dedicated and committed to their tasks. As such they can often be found going above and beyond what is required to ensure that the job is done to the best of their abilities.
- **Leadership Qualities:** With their natural inclination towards responsibility and reliability, Capricorns often make excellent leaders. They are capable of taking charge, setting goals and motivating others to achieve collective objectives.

- **Organizational Skills:** Capricorns possess remarkable organizational skills. They are adept at planning, structuring and executing projects efficiently. This makes them excellent managers and coordinators.
- **Practical and Analytical Mindset:** A practical and analytical approach to problems is another hallmark of Capricorns. They are able to assess situations logically and come up with realistic, workable solutions.
- **Ambitious and Goal-Oriented:** Their ambition drives them to set high goals for themselves and their determination ensures they persist until these goals are achieved. This trait often leads them to top positions within their chosen fields.
- **Dependability:** Capricorns are known for their dependability. Colleagues and superiors know they can rely on them to get the job done, meet deadlines and uphold commitments.
- **Attention to Detail:** They have a keen eye for detail, which is crucial in many professional settings. This meticulousness ensures that their work is of high quality and accuracy.
- **Patience and Persistence**: Capricorns are patient and not deterred by challenges or setbacks. They are willing to put in the time and effort required to see a project through to completion.
- **Professionalism:** They maintain a high level of professionalism in the workplace. Capricorns are respectful, tactful and usually adhere to workplace etiquette, contributing positively to the work environment.

- **Financial Acumen:** Many Capricorns have a natural understanding of financial matters, making them adept in roles that involve budgeting, finance, or resource management.

In summary, the combination of a strong work ethic, leadership, organizational skills and a practical mindset makes Capricorns highly effective and respected in the workplace. These traits not only help them excel in their careers but also often lead them to take on influential roles in their professional environments.

CHALLENGES CAPRICORNS MAY FACE IN THEIR CAREERS AND STRATEGIES TO OVERCOME THEM

While Capricorns have many strengths that make them successful in their professional lives, like all individuals, they also face certain challenges in their careers. Understanding these challenges and adopting effective strategies to overcome them can help Capricorns maximize their potential and achieve greater satisfaction in their work.

- **Tendency to Be Workaholic;** Capricorns' strong work ethic can sometimes lead to workaholism. They may struggle to maintain a healthy work-life balance, which can lead to burnout. Actively schedule downtime and hobbies outside of work. Prioritize tasks and delegate when necessary to manage workload effectively.

- **Difficulty in Adapting to Change;** Capricorns often prefer traditional methods and may resist new ways of working or innovative approaches, which can hinder adaptability in a fast-evolving workplace. Embrace a mindset of continuous learning and be open to new ideas. Participating in workshops or training sessions can help stay updated with current trends.

- **Reluctance to Express Emotions;** Capricorns might find it challenging to express their feelings, especially in a work environment. This can sometimes lead to misunderstandings with colleagues or a perception of being too distant. Work on communication skills. Especially in

47

expressing appreciation, concerns, or feedback in a constructive manner.

- **Risk-Averse Nature;** Their cautious nature might lead them to avoid taking necessary risks that could lead to significant professional growth. Learn to evaluate risks logically and understand that calculated risks are an essential part of career growth. Seek advice from mentors to gain different perspectives.

- **Perfectionism;** Capricorns' attention to detail can turn into perfectionism. This can lead to unnecessary stress and unrealistic expectations of themselves and others. Set realistic standards and timelines. Practice self-compassion and recognize that making mistakes is part of the learning process.

- **Struggle with Networking;** Their reserved nature can sometimes make networking and building professional relationships challenging. Set specific networking goals and attend industry events. Practice conversation starters and follow up with contacts regularly.

- **Overemphasis on Career Goals;** Capricorns' focus on career success might lead to neglecting other aspects of life, impacting personal relationships and overall well being. Cultivate interests and relationships outside of work. Recognize the importance of a holistic approach to life for long-term success and happiness.

- **Difficulty Accepting Help;** Their independent nature can make it hard for them to seek or accept help, which can limit their growth and increase workload. Acknowledge the benefits of collaboration and teamwork. Be open to support from colleagues and superiors.

In summary, by recognizing these obstacles and implementing strategies to tackle them, Capricorns can enhance their satisfaction and performance in their careers. By finding a balance between their inclinations and adaptability they can effectively leverage their strengths while mitigating challenges along their professional journey.

As we conclude this chapter one thing becomes clear. For Capricorns, careers and money are more than measures of success or stability. They serve as channels through which they express their identity, values and aspirations. Recognizing this deeper connection empowers Capricorns to make choices that bring fulfillment in these aspects of life.

CHAPTER 5:
SELF-IMPROVEMENT

In this chapter we will dive into the world of Capricorns and their unwavering dedication to self improvement. Capricorns, who are born under the ambitious sign of the mountain goat are renowned for their determination, practicality and strong work ethic. They possess a set of qualities that drive them towards growth and development.

Within the pages of this chapter we will explore both the strengths and weaknesses associated with this zodiac sign. We will shed light on how Capricorns harness their characteristics to achieve their goals. We'll delve into their determination, practical mindset and deep sense of responsibility while examining how these traits contribute to their journey of self improvement. Moreover we will address challenges that Capricorns might encounter such as stubbornness, pessimism and the quest for work life balance. This chapter provides insights and strategies for Capricorns to overcome these obstacles and further enhance their growth.

Join us on a voyage of discovery as we explore the qualities that make Capricorns so adept, at self improvement. We'll also uncover strategies they can employ to sustain their pursuit of excellence in all facets of life.

PERSONAL GROWTH AND DEVELOPMENT

Personal growth and self improvement play an important role in the lives of individuals born under the zodiac sign Capricorn. Those represented by the ambitious mountain goat are recognized for their steadfastness, responsibility and strong work ethic. They possess an inclination to strive for success and are motivated by their desire to conquer life's challenges. Let's delve deeper into the topic of growth and development, for Capricorns.

- **Goal Setting and Achievement**; Capricorns excel at setting goals and accomplishing them. Their practicality allows them to achieve highly in many aspects of their lives. Personal growth often

51

begins with identifying ambitions followed by creating plans to attain them. Continuously striving to better themselves and their circumstances is ingrained in their nature.

- **Embracing Discipline;** Discipline serves as a foundation for growth in Capricorn's lives. They possess an ability to remain focused on their goals despite challenges or distractions that may arise along the way. This enables them to develop self control and resilience during times.

- **Nurturing Patience;** While Capricorns are renowned for their adaptive nature they also recognize the value of patience when it comes to growth. They understand that achieving success often requires time and are willing to patiently wait. This helps them develop resilience and maintain a sense of purpose when faced with setbacks.

- **Embracing Change;** While they may have a preference for tradition and stability they acknowledge that growth often necessitates adapting to circumstances and seizing opportunities. As such, Capricorns strike a balance between their caution and a willingness to take calculated risks when needed.

- **Developing Emotional Intelligence;** Although Capricorns are commonly perceived as reserved and pragmatic, growth for them also entails nurturing intelligence. One must learn how to express their emotions, empathize with others feelings and cultivate connections with people. This not only leads to meaningful relationships but also enhances their leadership abilities by enabling them to better understand and motivate those they work with.

- **Balancing Work and Personal Life**; Capricorn's strong work ethic can occasionally cause an imbalance between their work and personal lives. It is important for them to find ways to strike an equilibrium ensuring they don't neglect their well being, relationships or leisure time.

- **Continuous learning;** Capricorns are often open to receiving mentorship and help. They recognize the importance of learning from those who have already achieved success in their fields. Engaging with mentors can expedite their personal growth journey and help them to make informed decisions.

To summarize Capricorns believe that personal growth and development require a combination of discipline, patience, ambition and adaptability. They are motivated by their aspiration to succeed and are willing to put in the effort to achieve their goals. By embracing change, nurturing intelligence and seeking balance, Capricorns can continue to evolve and flourish both personally and professionally.

HARNESSING CAPRICORN STRENGTHS AND OVERCOMING WEAKNESSES

Capricorns possess a unique set of strengths and weaknesses that shape their personality and influence their approach to life. To achieve personal growth and success, it's essential for individuals born under this zodiac sign to harness their strengths while actively working on overcoming their weaknesses. Here's a closer look at how Capricorns can do just that.

HARNESSING CAPRICORN STRENGTHS

- **Determination and Ambition**: Capricorns are renowned for their unwavering determination and ambition. They set their sights high and are willing to put in the necessary effort to achieve their goals. To harness this strength effectively, Capricorns should continuously set and update their goals. Both short-term and long-term. By maintaining a clear vision and a solid work ethic, they can steadily climb the ladder of success.

- **Discipline**: Capricorns are masters of discipline. This enables them to stay focused and organized. They should leverage this strength by creating structured routines and schedules. By adhering to a well-organized plan, they can efficiently manage their time and tasks. Ultimately leading to increased productivity and personal growth.

- **Practicality**: Capricorns possess a practical mindset that allows them to make sound decisions. This strength can be used to their advantage by thoroughly analyzing situations, weighing pros and cons and considering the long-term consequences. This will help them avoid impulsive decisions and steer clear of unnecessary risks.

- **Patience**: Patience is a valuable asset for Capricorns. They should embrace this strength when faced with setbacks or delays in their pursuits. Recognizing that success often requires time and persistence can help them maintain a positive attitude and stay committed to their goals.

- **Reliability**: Capricorns are known for their dependability and strong sense of responsibility. They should continue to cultivate this strength by fulfilling their commitments and supporting others when needed. Building trust and maintaining a solid reputation for reliability can open doors to new opportunities and collaborations.

OVERCOMING CAPRICORN WEAKNESSES:

- **Stubbornness**: Capricorns' determination can sometimes border on stubbornness. To overcome this weakness, they should practice flexibility and be open to alternative viewpoints. Learning to adapt to changing circumstances and considering different perspectives can help them make more well-rounded decisions.

- **Pessimism**: Capricorns may have a tendency to focus on potential obstacles or setbacks. To overcome this weakness, they should work on developing a more optimistic outlook. Practicing gratitude, positive affirmations and visualizing success can help them cultivate a more positive mindset.

- **Work-Life Balance**: Capricorns' strong work ethic can lead to neglecting their personal lives. To address this weakness, they should prioritize self-care, leisure activities and spending quality time with loved ones. Setting boundaries and allocating time for relaxation is crucial for maintaining a healthy work-life balance.

- **Rigidity**: Capricorns may sometimes become too rigid in their routines and expectations. They can overcome this weakness by consciously introducing variety into their lives, trying new experiences and embracing change as a natural part of personal growth.

- **Fear of Failure**: Capricorns' fear of failure can hold them back from taking necessary risks. To conquer this weakness, they should remind themselves that failure is often a stepping stone to success. Embracing setbacks as valuable learning experiences can help them build resilience and face challenges with greater confidence.

To sum up Capricorns have excellent qualities that when effectively utilized can lead to significant personal growth and success. However it's crucial for them to address their weaknesses in order to become rounded individuals. By embracing change, practicing flexibility and maintaining a positive mindset, Capricorns can strike a balance between their strengths and weaknesses. In doing so the potential for success and fulfillment becomes limitless.

CHAPTER 6:
THE YEAR AHEAD

Welcome to a fresh new chapter, where we are about to delve into events and influences that will shape the lives of Capricorn individuals in the year ahead. We will analyze how celestial movements can impact aspects of Capricorn's lives including matters of the heart, relationships, career prospects, finances, health, wellness, personal growth, self discovery and much more. By understanding these currents and harnessing their energies you can make better decisions and embark on a journey of growth, fulfillment and success in the year ahead. Join us as we unveil the roadmap for the year ahead!

HOROSCOPE GUIDE FOR CAPRICORN INDIVIDUALS

Welcome, Capricorn! As you embark on the journey of the year ahead, the stars, bodies and planets have aligned to provide insights into the opportunities and challenges that may come your way. Here's your horoscope guide for the upcoming year.

- **Aries (March 21 - April 19) -** Career and Ambition, Your ambition and strong work ethic will shine. During this time your career is in focus. New responsibilities or considering a change will be apparent. Keep your goals clear, stay disciplined and don't be afraid to seek mentorship. Ultimately your determination will pave the way for profound, professional success.

- **Taurus (April 20 - May 20) -** Finances and Stability, Financial stability is a key theme for Capricorns this year. It's a good time to review your budget and make wise investments. Your practical nature will help you make sound financial decisions. Be patient and stay focused on long-term financial goals.

- **Gemini (May 21 - June 20) - Communication and Relationships -** Communication skills will be essential in your relationships this year. Be open and honest with your loved ones. Make an effort to understand their perspectives. Strengthening your connections will bring harmony and growth in your personal life.

- **Cancer (June 21 - July 22) - Self-Care and Well-Being-** Capricorns, remember to take care of your physical and emotional well-being. Your hardworking nature can sometimes lead to neglecting self-care. Prioritize relaxation, exercise and a balanced diet to maintain your health and vitality.

- **Leo (July 23 - August 22) - Creativity and Hobbies -** This year, explore your creative side, Capricorn. Engage in hobbies or activities that bring you joy and allow your imagination to flourish. Creative outlets can provide a much-needed escape from the daily grind.

- **Virgo (August 23 - September 22) - Relationships and Partnerships -** Your practicality and attention to detail will be assets in your relationships. If you're in a committed partnership, focus on teamwork and communication. Single Capricorns may find opportunities for meaningful connections. Keep an open heart.

- **Libra (September 23 - October 22) - Learning and Growth -** This year, expand your knowledge and skills, Capricorn. Whether it's through formal education, self-study, or workshops. Embrace opportunities for personal growth. Your willingness to learn will lead to new horizons.

- **Scorpio (October 23 - November 21) - Family and Home Life -** Family matters will be a priority in the coming year. Spend quality time with loved ones, and resolve any lingering family issues. Creating a harmonious home environment will bring you comfort and peace.

- **Sagittarius (November 22 - December 21) - Networking and Social Connections -** Now is time to expand your social circle. Networking can lead to exciting opportunities both personally and professionally. Attend social events and connect with like-minded individuals who share your goals and values.

- **Capricorn (December 22 - January 19) - Self-Reflection and Goal Setting** - As a Capricorn, this is the perfect time to reflect on your life path and set new goals. Take stock of your achievements and make adjustments as needed. Your determination will drive you towards success in your endeavors.

- **Aquarius (January 20 - February 18) - Travel and Adventure** - Consider planning a trip or an adventure, Capricorn. Break away from routine and explore new horizons. Travel can broaden your perspective and bring fresh inspiration to your life.

- **Pisces (February 19 - March 20) - Finances and Investments** - Financial opportunities may come your way this year. Consider investments or financial strategies that align with your long-term goals. Your practical approach will serve you well in managing your resources.

Ultimately as a Capricorn, your strong sense of discipline and ambition will continue to drive you towards success in various aspects of your life. Remember to balance your determination with self-care and nurturing your personal relationships. With the guidance of the stars, you can make the most of the year ahead and continue your journey towards personal growth and fulfillment.

KEY ASTROLOGICAL EVENTS AND THEIR IMPACT ON CAPRICORN

Throughout the year there are events that can shape your experiences and opportunities. Let's take a look at some events and how they can potentially influence Capricorn individuals.

- **Saturn Transits**; Saturn, being your ruling planet, holds a significant sway over your life as it moves through different signs and houses in your birth chart. These transits can bring both challenges and rewards. Saturn's influence often tests your patience, determination and commitment to your goals. However it also presents an opportunity for long term growth and maturity. Embrace the lessons Saturn teaches you. You'll emerge stronger and more resilient.

- **Jupiter Transits**; Jupiter, known as the planet of expansion and growth has the potential to bring opportunities and abundance to Capricorns during its transits through signs. This could manifest as career advancements, personal development breakthroughs or exciting travel prospects. Seize the chance to broaden your horizons by taking calculated risks and exploring possibilities.

- **New Moon and Full Moon Phases**; New Moons and Full Moons hold significance for Capricorns too. New Moons represent starts filled with intentions— for setting goals or initiating new projects. Full Moons on the hand often bring about a sense of culmination and clarity. It's important to pay attention to these phases as they can assist you in aligning your actions with your aspirations.

- **Solar and Lunar Eclipses**; Eclipses have the potential to be moments in your life for a Capricorn like yourself. Solar eclipses can signify beginnings while lunar eclipses often indicate endings and emotional revelations. These celestial events have the power to trigger shifts in aspects of your life such as career, relationships or personal beliefs. It's advisable to be prepared for changes and remain adaptable during eclipse seasons.

- **Mercury Retrograde**; When Mercury goes retrograde it can affect communication, technology and travel for everyone including Capricorn individuals like yourself. During these times it is crucial to double check plans, avoid signing contracts and practice patience when misunderstandings arise. This period can be utilized for introspection or revisiting projects.

- **Mars and Venus Transits**; Mars symbolizes action while Venus represents relationships. When these two planets transit through signs aligned with yours it can enhance your assertiveness. Take advantage of these periods by engaging in networking opportunities or pursuing endeavors that align with your goals.

- **Capricorn Season;** The period from December to January marks Capricorn season. A time specifically dedicated to you shining brightly. With the Sun in your sign, during this time frame you are bestowed with confidence and determination that empowers you further. Take advantage of this time to set goals, acknowledge your achievements and plan your path for the year.

- **Other planets;** Pay attention to the movements of planets, like Uranus, Neptune and Pluto. These extended transits can bring about changes in society that might indirectly affect your life. Stay adaptable and open minded during these periods allowing your perspectives to evolve.

Remember that astrology serves as a tool for self awareness and guidance but does not determine your fate. Your choices and actions ultimately shape your destiny. By staying aware of these events and their potential influences you can make informed decisions and navigate through life's challenges, with wisdom and grace as a Capricorn. Now let's explore some key areas of interest and how they will be affected in the upcoming year.

LOVE AND RELATIONSHIPS

For those born under the sign of Capricorn, the astrological events that occur throughout the year can have an impact on their love lives and relationships. It is important to take note of the following happenings.

- **Venus in Capricorn**; As Venus enters your sign in the year Capricorn it enhances your charm and magnetism. Utilize this period to connect with your loved ones. Strengthen existing relationships and embark on romantic ventures. Your practical approach to love can lead to commitments.

- **Jupiter in Pisces;** During this phase Jupiter moves into Pisces, which's your sign. This will influence your partnerships and romantic endeavors. It has the potential to bring growth and expansion in your relationships by encouraging you to explore horizons with a partner. Be open to deepening connections and embracing the aspects of love.

- **Mercury Retrograde in Air Signs;** This period of Mercury retrograde might introduce communication challenges within your relationships. Be patient and mindful of choosing your words to avoid misunderstandings. Take this opportunity to revisit issues with compassion and a hearted approach.

- **Saturn Retrograde** Saturn, which is your ruling planet retrogrades in Aquarius, during this time period. This urges you to reassess your commitments and responsibilities within your relationships. Take this time to reflect on yourself. Ensure that your partnerships align with your long term goals. Don't avoid addressing any issues that need attention.

- **The New Moon in Capricorn;** Now is an opportunity for you to set intentions for your love life. Take a moment to think about your desires and goals in relationships Capricorn and then take steps throughout the year to bring them into reality.

FINANCES

The astrological events of the year have implications for your career and financial situation as a Capricorn. Pay attention to these milestones;

- **Saturn in Aquarius;** As Saturn continues its journey through Aquarius it emphasizes innovation and unconventional approaches in your life. Embrace change and explore progressive ideas to advance in your career.
- **Jupiter in Aries;** Jupiter's transit through Aries can ignite your ambition. This period might bring opportunities for career growth and expansion. Take initiative, make calculated risks and seize chances to climb up the ladder.
- **Mercury Retrograde;** During this period of Mercury retrograde you may encounter communication challenges at work. Make sure to double check the specifics, avoid any misunderstandings and concentrate on improving projects to increase efficiency.
- **Solar and Lunar Eclipses;** Be prepared for changes and opportunities. It's important to adapt

your strategies and consider investments that align with your long term goals. Additionally the Lunar Eclipse will again put a spotlight on financial matters. This might prompt you to reevaluate your stability and make adjustments to secure your future.

HEALTH AND WELLNESS

The astrological events throughout the year can have an impact on the health and well being of Capricorn individuals. Here's what you can do to maintain your well being while minimizing any negative effects;

- **Uranus movements -** Uranus may create tension between your desire for structure and the need for innovation. To reduce stress make sure to balance your work routines with opportunities for relaxation and creativity.
- **Venus is in Capricorn;** Now it's a time for self care. Focus on pampering yourself and improving both your emotional well being. You may want to consider trying out a fitness routine or wellness practice as a way of enhancing our health.
- **Jupiter's influence in Pisces:** This may encourage growth as well as emotional development. Discover the benefits of practicing mindfulness, meditation or seeking therapy to support your emotional wellbeing.

Capricorn individuals have the opportunity to embrace events throughout the year to foster growth and self discovery. Here's how you can make the most of the year;

- **Saturn Retrograde;** During Saturn's retrograde phase take time to reflect on your long term goals. Reassess your commitments, career path and personal aspirations to ensure they align with yourself.

- **Jupiter in Aries;** Embrace the energy of Jupiter in Aries as an opportunity to broaden your horizons. Take on new challenges, explore your passions and dare to step out of your comfort zone.

- **Mercury Retrograde in Earth Signs;** Utilize this period of Mercury retrograde for self reflection and revisiting projects. Examine areas in your life that require refinement and improvement.

- **New Moon in Capricorn;** Set intentions for the upcoming year. Focus on growth, self discovery and pursuing your goals with determination and clarity.

As we come to a close in our exploration of what lies for Capricorn individuals in terms of astrology it becomes clear that the stars have aligned to present a blend of opportunities and challenges. Your unwavering determination and practicality which are qualities of being a Capricorn will serve as your companions as you navigate through celestial currents.

In the tapestry of the universe Capricorn, your unique journey tells a story of ambition, determination and development. Remember that astrology serves as a guiding light. It is ultimately your choices and actions that shape your destiny. With the insights gained from this chapter you can embark on the year with wisdom, bravery, knowing that the stars are there to support you on your path, towards fulfillment and success.

As you enter into this year embrace opportunities as they arise and face challenges head on while letting your Capricorn spirit lead you towards reaching your potential. May both the journey itself be fulfilling as reaching the destination itself rewarding. May the stars continue to guide you along this path.

CHAPTER 7:
FAMOUS "CAPRICORN" PERSONALITIES

W elcome to the captivating realm of individuals, with the zodiac sign of Capricorn. In this chapter we embark on a voyage through the lives of people who share this astrological symbol. Capricorns are known for their determination, practicality and strong work ethic. Not surprisingly they have left a lasting impact on various domains such as history, entertainment, politics and more.

As we delve into the lives and accomplishments of these celebrated Capricorns we will explore the characteristics and qualities that define this zodiac sign. From their various pursuits to their influence on the world around them we will unravel the captivating stories of these exceptional individuals who truly embody what it means to be a Capricorn.

Whether you are a Capricorn seeking inspiration from your zodiac peers or simply intrigued by astrology's influence on personalities, this chapter promises an enlightening exploration of remarkable achievements and enduring legacies left behind by these iconic Capricorn figures. Join us as we embark on this journey into the captivating world of the Capricorn stars.

ELVIS PRESLEY

- Date of Birth: January 8, 1935.
- Brief Biography: Elvis Presley, often referred to as the "King of Rock and Roll," was a legendary American singer and actor. He rose to fame in the mid-1950s and became a cultural icon known for his charismatic performances and pioneering music.
- Capricorn Traits: Determination, ambition and discipline.
- Impact: Elvis revolutionized the music industry and left an enduring legacy. His influence on rock and pop music continues to be felt today.
- Personal Life: Elvis struggled with the pressures of fame and health issues. Sadly he passed away on August 16, 1977.

RICHARD NIXON

- Date of Birth: January 9, 1913.
- Brief Biography: Richard Nixon was the 37th President of the United States, serving from 1969 to 1974. He played a significant role in shaping American foreign policy during his tenure.
- Capricorn Traits: Ambition, practicality and resilience.
- Impact: Nixon's presidency was marked by achievements like opening relations with China but was also overshadowed by the Watergate scandal, leading to his resignation in 1974.
- Personal Life: Nixon's political career was marked by both success and controversy. He passed away on April 22, 1994.

BETSY ROSS

- Date of Birth: January 1, 1752.
- Brief Biography: Betsy Ross is credited with creating the first American flag with thirteen stars and thirteen stripes, representing the original colonies. She was a seamstress and a symbol of American patriotism.
- Capricorn Traits: Practicality, craftsmanship and attention to detail.
- Impact: Betsy Ross' contribution to American history as the flag's designer endures as a symbol of national pride.
- Personal Life: Betsy Ross was a skilled upholsterer and ran her own upholstery business in Philadelphia. She passed away on January 30, 1836.

GRETA THUNBERG

- Date of Birth: January 3, 2003.
- Brief Biography: Greta Thunberg is a Swedish environmental activist who gained international recognition for her efforts to combat climate change.
- Capricorn Traits: Determination, resilience and leadership.
- Impact: Greta's activism has sparked a global movement, raising awareness about climate change and advocating for urgent action.
- Personal Life: Greta continues her advocacy work and is recognized as a prominent voice for climate action.

MARLENE DIETRICH

- Date of Birth: December 27, 1901.
- Brief Biography: Marlene Dietrich was a German-American actress and singer known for her glamorous Hollywood career. She starred in iconic films such as "The Blue Angel" and "Destry Rides Again."
- Capricorn Traits: Ambition, elegance and discipline.
- Impact: Marlene's beauty and talent made her an international star. She challenged gender norms with her androgynous style and bold persona.
- Personal Life: Marlene had a long and successful career, but she also faced personal challenges. She passed away on May 6, 1992.

DAVID BOWIE

- Date of Birth: January 8, 1947.
- Brief Biography: David Bowie was a British musician and actor known for his innovative and ever-evolving music style. He was a pioneer of glam rock and experimented with various genres throughout his career.
- Capricorn Traits: Creativity, versatility and ambition.
- Impact: Bowie's contributions to music and fashion continue to influence artists across generations. His hits include "Space Oddity" and "Heroes."
- Personal Life: Bowie enjoyed a successful music career and acted in films. He passed away on January 10, 2016.

KIM JONG-UN

- Date of Birth: January 8, 1983.
- Brief Biography: Kim Jong-un is the Supreme Leader of North Korea, succeeding his father, Kim Jong-il. He has been a controversial figure in global politics, leading a reclusive regime.
- Capricorn Traits: Ambition, leadership and secrecy.
- Impact: Kim Jong-un's leadership has had a significant impact on North Korea's policies and international relations, often resulting in tensions.
- Personal Life: Much of Kim Jong-un's life remains shrouded in secrecy. His regime has been criticized for human rights abuses.

JOAN OF ARC

- Date of Birth: January 6, 1412.
- Brief Biography: Joan of Arc, also known as the Maid of Orleans, was a French military leader and a heroine of the Hundred Years' War. She played a crucial role in securing French victories.
- Capricorn Traits: Determination, courage and resilience.
- Impact: Joan of Arc's bravery and leadership inspired her troops and contributed to turning the tide of the war in favor of the French.
- Personal Life: Joan of Arc faced trials and was eventually executed by the English on May 30, 1431.

DOLLY PARTON

- Date of Birth: January 19, 1946.
- Brief Biography: Dolly Parton is a celebrated American singer, songwriter, and actress known for her country music career and hits like "Jolene" and "I Will Always Love You."
- Capricorn Traits: Determination, authenticity and creativity.
- Impact: Dolly's contribution to country music has earned her numerous awards, and her philanthropic efforts, including supporting literacy, have left a lasting impact.
- Personal Life: Dolly continues to perform and is an advocate for various charitable causes.

ROWAN ATKINSON

- Date of Birth: January 6, 1955.
- Brief Biography: Rowan Atkinson is a British comedian and actor famous for his roles in "Mr. Bean" and "Blackadder." His comedic talent has made him an international star.
- Capricorn Traits: Practicality, humor and versatility.
- Impact: Rowan Atkinson's iconic character, Mr. Bean, has entertained audiences worldwide for decades, making him one of the most recognized comedians.
- Personal Life: Rowan Atkinson continues to work in comedy and acting, delighting audiences with his wit and humor.

MARY TYLER MOORE

- Date of Birth: December 29, 1936.
- Brief Biography: Mary Tyler Moore was an American actress known for her roles in "The Mary Tyler Moore Show" and "The Dick Van Dyke Show." She was a beloved television icon.
- Capricorn Traits: Ambition, professionalism and charm.
- Impact: Mary Tyler Moore's talent and charm made her a beloved figure in television history. Her work paved the way for women in the entertainment industry.
- Personal Life: Mary Tyler Moore enjoyed a successful career but also faced personal challenges. She passed away on January 25, 2017.

FAYE DUNAWAY

- Date of Birth: January 14, 1941.
- Brief Biography: Faye Dunaway is an American actress known for her roles in iconic films like "Bonnie and Clyde" and "Network." She has received critical acclaim for her work.
- Capricorn Traits: Determination, elegance and versatility.
- Impact: Faye Dunaway's performances have earned her numerous awards, including an Academy Award for her role in "Network."
- Personal Life: Faye Dunaway continues to be a respected figure in the film industry.

The above, famous Capricorn individuals have all left their mark on various fields, showcasing the determination, ambition, and resilience. Such traits are the true characteristic of this zodiac sign. As we draw this chapter to a close it serves as a reminder of the enduring impact and significant contributions made by Capricorn individuals to society, culture and the world as a whole. Their narratives bear testament to the power of determination, hard work and an enduring spirit that characterizes those born under Capricorn's influence.

As we bid farewell to this chapter may you find inspiration and admiration in these personalities associated with Capricorn. Their legacies continue to radiate, serving as a reminder that with perseverance and practicality the stars are indeed attainable, for those born under this remarkable zodiac sign.

CONCLUSION

———— ✺ ————

As we conclude our exploration of the Capricorn star sign, it's first important to reflect on the key insights and themes that have emerged throughout our chapters. After this summary of chapters we will wrap up all that we have discovered and give some valuable takeaways.

Each chapter has delved deeply into different aspects of Capricorn, revealing a complex and multifaceted sign. Let's take a moment to summarize what we discover in each chapter.

- **Chapter 1: History and Mythology** - This chapter explored the historical and mythological roots of the Capricorn sign. We discovered how ancient civilizations perceived Capricorn and how these perceptions have evolved over time. This historical perspective provided a foundation for understanding the enduring traits and symbols associated with Capricorn.

- **Chapter 2: Love & Compatibility** - In this chapter, we examined the romantic side of Capricorn. We explored how Capricorn's qualities influence their love life and relationships. The chapter also provided insights into Capricorn's compatibility with other zodiac signs, offering guidance for harmonious partnerships.

- **Chapter 3: Friends And Family** - This chapter focused on the social and family aspects of

Capricorn. It delved into how Capricorns interact with friends and family. Furthermore we looked at their loyalty, protective nature and how they express love and support in close relationships.

- **Chapter 4: Career And Money** - Capricorn's professional life and financial management were the focus of this chapter. We explored how their traits like ambition, discipline and pragmatism shape their career choices and approach to finances.

- **Chapter 5: Self-Improvement** - Here, we delved into the ways Capricorns can pursue personal growth and self-improvement. The chapter provided strategies for Capricorns to leverage their strengths and address their challenges for a more fulfilling life.

- **Chapter 6: The Year Ahead** - This chapter provided a forward-looking analysis, offering predictions and guidance for Capricorns in the coming year. We discussed potential challenges and opportunities that await them in various aspects of life.

- **Chapter 7: Famous "Capricorn" Personalities** - In the final chapter, we explored the lives and achievements of famous Capricorn individuals. This chapter highlighted how Capricorn traits have manifested in these personalities. One can find inspiration and insights into the potential of this star sign.

In conclusion the journey through the world of Capricorn has been truly enlightening. It has revealed a star sign that possesses depth and diversity. From its ancient origins to its modern expressions, Capricorns embody a unique blend of discipline, ambition and practicality that sets them apart. As we bring this book to a close our hope is that readers have gained a deep understanding of Capricorn and are equipped with the knowledge to navigate the intricacies of this zodiac sign.

The central focus of this book is a profound exploration into the realm of Capricorn astrology. Throughout our exploration we have delved into many aspects such as history, mythology, personal relationships, career development and self improvement in order to unravel the multi-faceted nature of Capricorns. Our objective was to provide readers with insights into the strengths, challenges and potentials associated with being a Capricorn.

We stand by our commitment. We have successfully fulfilled it by examining each dimension of a Capricorn's life. From tracing their roots and unveiling symbolism to offering practical advice on love relationships, family dynamics, professional growth opportunities and much more. We have presented a well rounded perspective on what it means to be a Capricorn. Additionally our analysis of individuals born under this sign along with predictions for the upcoming year further enriches our understanding by showcasing how astrological traits can manifest in real world contexts.

The main takeaway we hope readers grasp is the depth and intricate nature of the Capricorn sign. Capricorns are not solely defined by ambition and discipline. They encompass resilience, loyalty and practical wisdom. Overall they possess a unique approach to facing life's challenges and embracing opportunities.

We encourage individuals who identify as Capricorns to embrace their qualities. Your strength, determination and practicality are assets that can lead to great accomplishments and to foster deep meaningful relationships. Your journey through life guided by these attributes is not only about success but also a testament to the enduring power of your signs' characteristics.

As we conclude this book, it has comprehensively delved into what it means to embody the essence of being a Capricorn. From ancient times until now Capricorns have proven themselves to be more than their star sign. Ultimately they are individuals with vibrant lives shaped by celestial influences yet firmly rooted, in the realities of our world. We sincerely hope that the wisdom and understanding you have gained here will serve as inspiration and guidance, for anyone looking to delve into this zodiac sign. Best wishes!

Subscribe To Sofia Visconti

As a subscriber you will receive a Free Gift + You wil be the first to hear about new books, articles and more exclusives **just for you**

Click Here

Or Visit Below:
https://www.subscribepage.com/svmyth

Or Simply Scan The Qr Code To Join

Made in the USA
Las Vegas, NV
14 December 2024

99216f69-3042-41b9-80a9-d809f169b5d2R01